EXPLORING
BUSINESS
AND
ECONOMICS

MONEY AND BANKING

FAMOUS FINANCIERS AND INNOVATORS

WORLD TRADE

THE STOCK MARKET

TAXES

THE ECONOMY

INVESTING YOUR MONEY

PERSONAL FINANCE

EXPLORING
BUSINESS
AND
ECONOMICS

World Trade

John Burgess

Chelsea House Publishers
Philadelphia

Frontis: **Military aircraft may be designed for a specific country, but often the parts used to make the planes are manufactured all over the globe—it's just one more way that trade ties the world together.**

CHELSEA HOUSE PUBLISHERS

EDITOR-IN-CHIEF Sally Cheney
DIRECTOR OF PRODUCTION Kim Shinners
PRODUCTION MANAGER Pamela Loos
ART DIRECTOR Sara Davis

Choptank Syndicate/Chestnut Productions

EDITORIAL Norman Macht and Mary Hull
PRODUCTION Lisa Hochstein
PICTURE RESEARCH Norman Macht

http://www.chelseahouse.com

First Printing

1 3 5 7 9 8 6 4 2

Library of Congress Cataloging-in-Publication Data

Burgess, John, 1957–
    World trade / John Burgess.
    p. cm. — (Exploring business and economics)
    ISBN 0-7910-6638-X (alk. paper)
1. International trade. 2. International economic relations. I. Title. II. Series.
HF1379.B87 2001
382—dc21   2001042512

Table of Contents

When people talk about world trade, they usually think of things such as steel, automobiles, and textiles. But movies are one of America's leading exports. Walt Disney's classic *Snow White* is recognized all over the world.

Bringing the World to You

You may not be a world traveler, but the chances are that your house is full of products that have ridden jets and freighters across oceans and continents to come to you.

Take your sneakers, for instance. They may have come from a factory in southern China. Your television set may be from across the border in Mexico. The shirts in your closet may be from Costa Rica. The car in your garage might have come from Korea, and the tangerines on your kitchen table are probably from Spain.

Countries have been trading since ancient times. But in the years since World War II, **trade** has boomed, tying the people of the globe together as never before. In 2000, the world's countries sold each other about $5 trillion worth of goods, up from $2 trillion in 1980. All over the world today factories and farms produce things for people thousands of miles away. Go to any port or big airport and you can see trade happening: ships steaming out of port bound for foreign countries, holds full of wheat grown by American farmers; machinery made by American factory workers; cargo jets flying in from foreign countries carrying loads of computer chips.

Economists and other people who study trade believe it is a big part of why the world today is, on average, a much wealthier place than it used to be. Trade allows each country to concentrate on making the things that it can make more cheaply than any other country, and then to sell them to the whole world. If a country has the right climate, land, raw materials, and work skills among its people to produce a

Top Ten Trading Partners of the United States in 2000

Country	Value of U.S. Trade with that Country (Imports plus Exports)
Canada	$406 billion
Mexico	$248 billion
Japan	$212 billion
China	$116 billion
Germany	$88 billion
Britain	$85 billion
South Korea	$68 billion
Taiwan	$65 billion
France	$50 billion
Singapore	$37 billion

Source: U.S. Census Bureau

When Christopher Columbus landed in the West Indies in 1492, he traded beads, glass, and other trinkets for food and gold. Bartering (trading) was the only way people bought and sold things for thousands of years.

particular product at a very low cost—those tasty Spanish tangerines, for example—the country will produce enough for its own people and extra to sell to other countries. From those countries it buys things that it can't make at a low price itself. In the end, both sides are better off.

Every four years the world's countries compete with each other in sports at the Olympic Games. In the same way, they compete in trade—only it happens every day. Each country works hard to build the best products at the lowest price, to get the world's business. That means having well-educated, hard-working employees and skillful managers. It means building good roads and ports to transport goods. It means having a stable government, without civil war or riots, so that people can focus on making things rather than fighting each other. Some countries focus on growing crops, others on building cars, and others on sewing clothes. Some countries may lead in a particular product, selling more than others, until another country overtakes them, just as happens in sports.

Because it can make people rich, trade is one of the driving forces of history. If you look back over the centuries, you'll often find that when a truly important event happens, trade is at the root of it.

Christopher Columbus discovered America, for instance, not because he was looking for new land to settle. He was looking for a shorter sea route to the Orient, a source of spices and other valuable things that Europeans couldn't grow themselves. He figured that if he found the new route, he could bring the goods to Europe at a lower cost than other ships that were taking the long route around the

Top U.S. Imports in 2000

Cars	$109.3 billion
Crude oil	$89.9 billion
Computer accessories	$75.5 billion
Computer chips	$48.3 billion
TVs, VCRs and other electronics	$21.0 billion
Toys, games, sporting goods	$21.0 billion
Fish and shellfish	$9.9 billion
Jewelry	$9.0 billion
Shingles and wallboard	$6.8 billion
Farm machinery	$4.1 billion
Blank recording cassettes	$2.4 billion
Chinaware and glassware	$2.4 billion

Source: U.S. Census Bureau

southern tip of Africa. He would become rich from trade with the East, or so he thought. But he never made it to the East. Instead, he found America—by accident.

More recently, trade was an important cause of the Persian Gulf War of 1991. The Middle Eastern country Iraq had invaded its neighbor Kuwait the year before, in part because it wanted the billions of dollars that Kuwait was making by pumping oil from the ground and loading it aboard tanker ships for sale to the rest of the world. The United States went to war to drive Iraq's army out of Kuwait. This was because it was friends with Kuwait, and because the U.S. government feared there would be trouble for its economy and that gas prices would go way up if a hostile country like Iraq controlled too much of the world's oil trade.

Although trade generally increases the total amount of wealth in the world, many people criticize it, because the

Top U.S. Exports in 2000

Computer chips	$60.0 billion
Communications equipment	$32.6 billion
Airliners and private aircraft	$22.6 billion
Cars	$16.7 billion
Pharmaceutical drugs	$14.3 billion
Plastics	$14.0 billion
Soybeans	$5.4 billion
Household appliances	$5.1 billion
Oil production equipment	$5.0 billion
Logs and lumber	$4.4 billion
Wheat	$3.5 billion
Rugs	$1.5 billion

Source: U.S. Census Bureau

wealth it creates is never shared equally. Some people actually become poorer due to trade. This happened to many Americans who worked at automobile factories in the 1980s. Japan had figured out ways to make small cars more cheaply than the United States could. They began selling those cars in the United States. As a result, American car factories lost business and had to cut thousands of jobs. Naturally, the people who lost their jobs because of increased Japanese car sales in the United States didn't like this trade very much.

Some countries also worry that if they depend on foreign factories for too many things, they will lose some of their independence and won't be able to fight back if they are attacked in a war. America now has very few shoe factories because it buys most of its shoes from abroad. This raises the question: who will make shoes for American soldiers if there is a war and the shoe trade is cut off?

Trade is often a very big issue during election campaigns. Some people say that the government shouldn't let the country increase what it buys from overseas, because foreign products can cost American jobs. They vote for politicians who promise to limit purchases from abroad, which are known as **imports.** But many other people believe that trade is good because it enables American consumers to buy low-cost products from abroad. They also say that it creates jobs in the United States because American factories can hire people to make products for sale abroad, called **exports.** These people vote for pro-trade politicians.

In general, the people and politicians who think that trade is good are prevailing. So you are likely to see more and more foreign products in your home in the years ahead.

And you may be surprised by what some countries trade with the rest of the world. One of the world's smallest

Most of the oil produced in the world is used in countries where it is not produced. No product is more vital to the global economy. Its flow may be interrupted by wars or political disputes.

countries became wealthy by selling old bird droppings! Birds have been nesting for thousands of years on the Pacific island of Nauru, 25 miles south of the equator. Over the years, their droppings formed a type of rock called phosphate, which is very useful in making fertilizer. People in Nauru mine the phosphates and load them on ships for sale to other countries that need fertilizer. That income (about $25 million in 1991) allows the island's 10,000 people to have one of the developing world's highest **standards of living.** The people of Nauru became almost entirely dependent on money from the phosphates, buying just about everything else they needed, including fresh water, from other countries. In the 1990s, with the phosphates running out, Nauru began looking for other ways to support its economy, such as international banking, which involoves helping foreigners move their money around the world.

In the United States, one of our hottest exports is entertainment, especially movies. In 1999, film studios took in almost $14 billion from overseas sales of movies, videos, and TV shows. This income created jobs at Hollywood film studios and helped pay those famous multimillion-dollar fees that big-name stars get. Action movies sell particularly well in just about all countries, because people everywhere seem to like the excitement of a quick-moving story and special effects. American studios are willing to spend a lot of money on these kinds of films because they know that people all over the world will pay to see them. But often American comedies don't do very well in other countries; people there may not understand American jokes.

Film studios in the United States get angry when people in foreign countries "pirate" the movies, that is, make copies of films without paying the studio anything. This is a form of theft. The U.S. government works closely with foreign governments to try to stamp out piracy, because it hurts the American film industry, and thus the nation's economy as a whole.

When you finish your schooling and get a job, it is more and more likely that your work will involve making things for people in other countries, or helping Americans buy foreign products. Creating software, building jetliners, selling European cars at a dealership, or working in a bank that lends money to foreign countries—any of these jobs would make you part of a world that is tied together by trade.

With 36,000 feet of sail, *Star Flyer* recalls the mid-19th century clipper ships that once hauled goods across the oceans with record speed.

How Trade Began

As far back as the Stone Age, people were already trading. A member of a tribe living near the ocean might walk inland a few miles and offer fish in exchange for things that people living in the hills had obtained. At first the trade used what's known as the **barter system**—trade without money. For example, 10 fish might be exchanged for one deerskin. Later money was invented to make exchanges like this easier. The person who had 10 fish and wanted a deerskin no longer had to go to the trouble of finding someone who had a deerskin but wanted 10 fish. Money could be used instead, because the person receiving it could then use it to buy something else.

As civilization developed, so did trade. In fact, historians say that trade is a big part of what made civilizations possible. Trade increased wealth and brought isolated peoples into contact with each other, resulting in exchanges of knowledge. As ancient societies became richer, some of their people were freed from work in the fields, giving them the time to invent things or learn to read and write. Civilization encouraged trade. As ancient governments minted coins, built roads, and cracked down on bandits,

The Boston Tea Party

The American Revolution happened because the colonists wanted democracy and self-government. But it also happened because they were upset with trade policy.

For years, the British government had been restricting and taxing the colonies' trade with the outside world. In 1767, for instance, the British parliament in London passed laws called the Townsend Acts, which put a tax on many items brought into the American colonies from abroad, such as glass, paint, and paper. That meant that colonists had to pay more for the goods, because the tax was added to the price.

The famous Boston Tea Party of 1773 took place because some colonists felt that Britain was giving unfair advantages to a British company that sold tea to the colonies, hurting American companies that were in the same business. So on the night of December 16, a group of colonists dressed up as Native Americans boarded three British ships in Boston Harbor, and threw crates of the British company's tea into the harbor. Britain responded by punishing the colonies. It closed the port of Boston to try to force the colonists to pay for the ruined tea. That only made more Americans think it was time to throw off British rule.

Stone weights in the shape of ducks were used 3,500 years ago to measure goods being bartered. The largest weighed two minas and the smallest 20 shekels.

people found it easier to transport goods long distances for sale. More and more people took the occupation of **trader,** someone who buys something in one place, transports it a long distance, and resells it to people who need it.

After China was united as an empire around 220 B.C., trade flourished inside the huge country, thanks to peace, roads, and good government. Ancient China also traded with the outside world. Chinese goods, especially silk, were carried by caravans of pack animals that crossed central Asia, and they were loaded into ships that sailed along the coast. Chinese people liked to buy glass objects that were made in the Mediterranean countries of the Roman Empire. They often traded silk for what they wanted—so much so, in fact, that the overland trails from China became known in Europe as "The Silk Road." The famous explorer Marco Polo, who set out from Venice in 1271 and eventually reached the palace of the emperor of China, was part of this trade.

Trade flourished in the Americas long before Europeans arrived. In the Aztec Empire that is now Mexico, merchants traveled across the countryside buying things such as cotton, jaguar skins, gold, and the brightly colored feathers of tropical birds. Guarded by armed men, the goods were transported great distances by caravans of people carrying loads on their backs. This trade made possible the existence of huge cities and teeming markets where thousands of people met daily to shop and gossip.

Trade also spread ideas. Arab traders visiting the islands that are now Indonesia helped to spread the Muslim religion. Technology moved around the world this way, too. The nicely glazed plates and cups that China sold to the world were so popular—even now we call them "chinaware"—that other countries adopted the Chinese production techniques and made chinaware for themselves.

In the age of the European explorers, trade became truly global. In 1492, Columbus reached America. Ships from Portugal sailed down the east coast of Africa, looking for a sea route to East Asia. They eventually rounded the tip of the continent and sailed up its east coast toward India. Over the years, trading centers were established all over the world. Merchants in coastal towns of Africa sold products to passing European ships; native peoples in Canada began to supply beaver skins to Europe for coats.

Europeans sometimes used their superior weapons to forcibly take over areas with which they wanted to trade. The British East India Company, which handled Britain's overseas trade, had its own army, and many of its ships were armed. For centuries trade between Africa, Europe, and the Americas also included the sale of human beings. Slave traders bought or took captives, who were shipped to the Americas, thousands of miles away from their homes, to work in mines, on plantations, and as servants.

Advances in transportation technology in the 1800s increased trade further. Shipyards built large and swift clipper ships. These many-sailed ships could speed products between China and Europe. The construction of railroads

A Roman Trade Ship

During the time of the Roman Empire, the Mediterranean Sea was busy with ships carrying goods from one corner of the empire to another: grain, animal skins, wine, even live animals captured in Africa for use in circuses. Different parts of the empire specialized in producing goods for other parts. Britain, for instance, sent out tin. Italy made wine, and Greece provided marble for grand buildings. The Roman government helped this trade by building about 50,000 miles of roads and keeping the sea free of pirates. It coined money that was accepted all over the empire.

In 1988 deep-sea explorer Dr. Robert Ballard discovered the wreckage of a Roman trading ship that had sunk in the Mediterranean Sea in 2,500 feet of water around the year 375 A.D. He gave it the name *Isis.* The wooden ship had been carrying hundreds of large jars called amphora, which lay scattered on the sea floor. A robot craft raised a number of the now-empty jars. Ballard believes that when the ship sank the jars were probably filled with olive oil and fish sauce being taken from North Africa for sale in the marketplaces of Italy.

More than 2,000 years ago, camels carried spices, silk, ivory, and other goods along the Silk Route, a 4,000 mile trek between China and the Mediterranean. Camels were called the ships of the desert.

allowed goods to move overland hundreds or even thousands of miles at low cost.

During the 1800s and early 1900s, European countries and the United States conquered parts of Africa and Asia and made them colonies, in part to control trade. The colonies tended to trade mainly with the country that conquered them, supplying raw materials and farm products in return for manufactured goods. Trade continued to expand as steamships and airplanes were invented and communications cables were strung across oceans. Now merchants could place orders from far-away countries in a matter of minutes. Before refrigeration, food had to be sold locally, because it would spoil on long trips. Later it became possible to send food long distances.

In the 1930s, the **Great Depression** sapped the economy of the world, putting millions of people out of work. Trade decreased dramatically because people had less money to spend on foreign products. Countries made things worse when they tried to protect their own factories and jobs from competition by refusing to let in goods from foreign countries. In 1930 the United States passed a law called the **Smoot Hawley Tariff Act** to keep out foreign products. Foreign countries responded by refusing to buy American products. In the end everyone was worse off. The hard times helped the rise to power of the people who started World War II—Adolf Hitler in Germany and military officers in Japan. They promised their peoples that they would govern firmly to put their economies back on track and create jobs again.

After Germany and Japan were defeated in 1945, most colonies of the world gained their independence. But now the **Cold War** affected patterns of trade. The world divided into two groups of competing countries, the **communist** countries led by the Soviet Union, and the non-communist countries led by the United States. Each group tended not to trade with the other. The Soviets sold goods to their allies, such as Poland and Cuba, while the United States traded with its friends, such as Britain, Japan, and the Philippines.

Soon the American-led group came up with a new idea: why not get rid of laws that limited trade and protected local industries? They sent ambassadors to meet and discuss how to do this. Gradually they began to open their markets to goods from their allies, believing that over time increasing trade would make them all richer and safer from enemies. Starting in the 1950s, the countries of western Europe began lowering **trade barriers** among themselves and trading more freely, creating what is today known as the **European Union.** The founders believed that if the European countries were firmly tied together by trade, they would be less likely to go to war with each other again.

In the 1960s, Japan began to rise as a major power in world trade. After perfecting new efficient methods of production, it made billions of dollars worth of cars, electronic equipment, and machinery and shipped them abroad. Products bearing the words "Made in Japan" began to show up all over the world. Other Asian countries, such as Singapore, South Korea, and China followed in Japan's footsteps, selling goods to the world. Their products caused major changes in the economy of the United States, as domestic car and electronics factories closed down because their business was damaged by low-cost imports from Asia.

In the final years of the 20th century, the Soviet Union collapsed and its former allies began trading with the rest of the world. Almost every country in the world began to take the view that expanding trade was the key to raising the standard of living. The United States, Canada, and Mexico signed the **North American Free Trade Agreement (NAFTA)** to merge their three countries into a single trading zone. The network of computers known as the **Internet** created new efficiencies in trade. People and companies could now buy and sell things instantly, by computer. If the product was a song or a copy of an old newspaper article, it could be delivered electronically over the Internet as well.

But not everyone prospered in this new system of trade. Many countries in Africa became poorer. They borrowed money from the outside world that they could not pay back.

Their sales to the world continued to depend on natural resources such as mineral ores, which did not bring in enough income to create prosperity. Civil wars broke out in some of these countries, destroying factories and disrupting farms. In general, these countries were unable to benefit from what became known as economic **globalization,** the tying of the world together through trade and communication. But they continued to try, because they knew that tying in with world markets had become the only real hope of prospering.

Meat, fish, and fruit like these Georgia peaches being hauled to market have become an important part of world trade as a result of modern refrigeration and the use of air freight. Half of all the food grown in the United States is exported.

Why Do People Trade?

Suppose that an American family decided one night that it was going to make everything for itself. They would grow their own vegetables, bake their own bread, raise cows, weave cloth, build a house, all without help from anyone else. The family wants to do this in order to be self-sufficient and not have to rely on anyone else. After all, who can say if the people who make the things we buy in the stores will keep doing it in the future? We usually don't even know who those people are.

Although the family might think it is a good idea to depend only on themselves, they would quickly become poor and frustrated. They wouldn't have any idea how to do all these complicated jobs. How would they build a complete house, designing it themselves, making and installing all of its complicated heating, plumbing, and wiring systems? How would they make shingles, air conditioners, and linoleum tiles? The family would end up at best with a drafty log cabin. Then there would be the problem of food. To make bread, they would have to grow the wheat themselves and do their own milling and baking. And what about a car? The family would probably quickly recognize that it could never hope to have one. It wouldn't be able to make steel and plastic, and besides, it might not have any oil deposits on its land. The family would have to use a horse, or just walk.

Many thousands of years ago, people recognized that their lives would be more prosperous if they specialized in making just a few products, the ones that they could make better than other people. Economists call this the law of **comparative advantage.** On the whole, the most wealth will be created, they say, if people focus on what they do best.

People in Scotland, for instance, are among the world's best at producing wool. They have the cool climate that sheep like and wide open spaces for grazing. Over the centuries, Scottish people have learned how to raise sheep that produce fine-quality wool. So the Scots often become wealthy from wool. It would make no sense for them to try to grow coconuts. Imagine what would happen if someone got that idea: the trees would die immediately in Scotland's harsh climate. That job is better done by people in tropical places like the Pacific island of Fiji, which has the soil and climate in which coconuts thrive, and the people who have learned how to make a coconut tree live long and produce the maximum number of coconuts. So Scots and Fijians stay out of each other's specialty businesses. When they need what the other makes, world trade provides it.

All over the world, countries take that approach. The United States has many specialties, including computers: the Silicon Valley area of California is crowded with companies turning out computer software and hardware. Germany produces luxury cars, such as the Mercedes and the BMW. Saudi Arabia produces a lot of oil. In Thailand, a big specialty is rice. This doesn't mean that these are the only countries that make these products. Countries constantly compete with others. Britain, for instance, makes software that competes with the United States. Japan makes luxury cars that compete with German models.

There are two basic philosophies about the best way for countries to regulate the buying and selling of one another's products. One is called **free trade** and basically means not

Illegal Trade

Not all of the world's trade is legal. Drugs such as cocaine and heroin flow in huge quantities from country to country, despite the efforts of police to stop them. But legal or not, this trade follows many of the same patterns of ordinary trade.

For instance, countries specialize in certain drugs. The South American nation of Colombia has lax law enforcement and excellent soil and climate for growing the coca plants that are used to make cocaine. So it grows a lot of them. The United States lacks the conditions for growing coca, so American drug users turn to imports. The price of cocaine goes up and down depending on supply. If bad weather or interception of shipments by police cuts off the supply, the prices that drug users pay go up. And the dollars that flow to Colombia from the United States to pay for the drugs makes some people in that country—the drug lords—very rich.

When a disease hits a crop, the effects are felt far beyond the farmer's field. American farms produce $6 billion worth of wheat a year, much of it for export. In 2000 a wheat disease threatened the crop in the western United States. Eighty countries ban the importing of wheat from a diseased area.

to regulate it at all. In this system, governments let goods move freely to whatever country wants to buy them. The other philosophy is called **protectionism.** In this approach, foreign products are kept out of a country because people worry that their sale will harm the country's own industries and destroy jobs.

No country uses either system exclusively; every country is a mix. The United States tends to believe more in free

trade than protectionism, letting a wide assortment of foreign products into the country, even if that means hard
times for some American factories. People who believe in
free trade say it means that low-cost, high-quality products
will be available in American stores. Letting foreign products in, the free traders say, also means that American-
made products continue to improve. This is because
companies in the United States must improve their products or risk losing customers to better foreign products.
Free traders admit that some Americans may lose their jobs
to foreign competition, but they believe that these people
can find new jobs in companies that make things that can
compete against foreign products. In the end, free traders
believe the country will be better off by concentrating on
making only what it makes better than other countries, and
closing factories that can't stand up to the foreign products.

Many Asian and European countries favor protectionism
more than the United States does. They prefer to shield
local factories from foreign competition. They believe that
this will insure that local people have jobs and will give
newly built local factories time to modernize and become
strong and competitive. These countries are a bit like the
family that wants to be self-reliant. They want to have their
own steel plants, their own farms, and their own airlines,
rather than relying on foreign countries to provide them.
This would make them more secure in times of war.
Sometimes they also think that certain jobs should be
preserved because they are part of a way of life. Would
France be France, they ask, if it didn't have pretty little
villages and family farms making cheese and raising cows?
Many people in France say the answer is no, so the
French government tries to protect these farms from
foreign competition.

Many economists say that countries that adopt the pro-tectionist approach pay a price. The country may feel more proud and secure, but its citizens must pay more for goods than they would otherwise. Such people believe the greater price is worth it for being shielded from the ups and downs of the world economy. If the outside world is hit by an economic slow-down, a protectionist country won't feel it as much as one that is fully plugged in to the world economy.

Protectionist countries have many ways to restrict the number of foreign products sold in their stores. One is to impose a **tariff,** a tax on a foreign product, collected when it enters the country. The merchant importing the product usually passes on the tariff to the consumer in the form of a higher price in the store. The higher price means that people buy fewer foreign products. If the tariff is set high enough, merchants won't bother importing the foreign goods at all. Another way to keep out foreign products is to create a **quota.** A rule might be enacted saying that only 100,000 cars from a certain country can be imported. Quotas tend to raise prices, because of the law of supply and demand—if something is in short supply, its price goes up. During the 1980s, when there was a quota limiting how many Japanese cars could enter the United States, dealers often raised the prices on Japanese models by a thousand dollars or more.

But sometimes a country doesn't like to admit that it is trying to keep out foreign products—the world in general, after all, favors free trade. So the government might find a sneakier way to keep a product out. If it wants to keep out foreign foods, for instance, it might declare that it is afraid of dangerous parasites entering the country in for-eign food and require that all shipments of foods go through extensive testing at the border. If that testing takes so long that the food spoils, merchants will stop trying to bring it in. In other cases, ordinary people in a country might decide that it is unpatriotic to buy foreign goods. Many American manufacturers, in fact, try to appeal to protectionist feelings by putting the words "Made in America"

Smugglers

Ever since governments began putting controls on the flow of products thousands of years ago, smugglers have been finding ways to beat those controls. Whether they are like Han Solo of the Star Wars movies or the notorious Colombian drug runner Pablo Escobar, smugglers make their living by sneaking things across borders and selling them.

Sometimes the products are illegal, like drugs, explosives, or ivory (general trade in ivory has been banned in an attempt to protect elephants). In the 1920s alcohol was outlawed in the United States and smugglers made fortunes by secretly bringing it into the country from Canada and elsewhere. In other cases, the products are legal, but smugglers are trying to avoid paying taxes. Britain, for instance, puts very high taxes on cigarettes in order to discourage people from smoking. So smugglers buy cigarettes in other countries where taxes are low and sneak them into Britain, sometimes hiding them in special compartments in vehicles. People buy the smuggled cigarettes for around half of the $6 or so that they would pay for a regular pack. Smugglers can afford to price the cigarettes cheaply because they aren't paying the taxes.

Governments try to stop smuggling by checking the baggage of visitors at airports and patrolling their country's coastlines to watch for smugglers' boats. But, as long as people can make money from smuggling, it will never be stopped completely.

on their goods. They hope this will make American shoppers favor their goods over foreign ones.

Protectionist countries may also control how foreign citizens can invest money in their economies. For instance, they might make it hard for foreigners to buy shares in local companies. They fear that if foreigners control those companies, they might make decisions that are not in the local interest. In wartime, for instance, foreign-owned television stations might broadcast information favorable to the enemy.

Since their systems are so different, protectionist countries and free trade countries often get into arguments. The basic problem is that protectionist countries generally want to make money by selling products to other countries, but they don't want to buy from them. Free trade countries say that's unfair. They want to sell their products to the protectionist countries.

Whether a country favors free trade or protectionism depends in part on the balance of political power between different groups within it. **Labor unions,** organizations that promote the rights of workers, often criticize free trade, because if foreign products put an American factory out of business union members there will lose their jobs. Unions also point out that workers in foreign countries are often paid very low wages, work in unsafe conditions, and don't have the rights to form unions. They say it is unfair for companies to exploit their workers that way. Many environmental groups also oppose unrestricted free trade. They contend that it leads people in developing countries to build factories that pollute the air and to chop down forests as they scramble to make products that the industrial world will buy. These groups say that the United States should practice what they call **fair trade** and have policies that consider not just whether a product has the lowest

Nicaragua jeans factory: American manufacturers of clothing and shoes have moved most of their production to countries like Nicaragua, where labor costs are lower. To see where a product was made, look at the label.

possible price, but the impact on jobs and the environment as well.

The executives of some companies favor free trade, because they want to save money when their companies make products. If they can produce something in a foreign country where workers are paid only 10 dollars a day, and then ship it back to the United States, they would often rather do it there than at home, where they might have to pay 10 dollars an hour. They point out that though the wages overseas may sound low to Americans, they seem very high to the local people, who flock to the factories and improve their lives by taking the jobs. These companies lobby for lower trade barriers, so that they can ship the goods they make abroad back into the United States for sale.

Other companies, however, prefer to keep their plants at home. They sometimes lobby for keeping trade barriers high to limit the entry of competing foreign products. They may argue that the competition is unfair, that the foreign products are priced low—not because they were made more efficiently but because a foreign government is giving a **subsidy,** a kind of financial aid, to the foreign company. The U.S. steel industry, for instance, has long pressed the federal government to protect it from what it calls unfair competition by foreign companies.

For many years now, the United States has bought more from the world than it sells to it. In 2000, our sales to the world totaled about $1.068 trillion, but our purchases were at $1.438 trillion. The shortfall, called the **trade deficit,** totaled about $370 billion.

This means that the United States is like a family that spends more than it earns. The family may have a very high standard of living, with a big-screen TV in the den and a fancy car in the garage, but it has to borrow money to keep living this way. In trade, this money comes from foreigners, who lend America money by investing their spare cash in American companies and financial markets.

Other countries, such as Japan, have a **trade surplus.** This means that they sell the world more than they buy. They are like families that spend less than they make. The difference is put in the bank. But the standard of living of this family isn't as high as it might be, because it's not spending all of its money.

Some American politicians and economists say that having deficits year after year means that the U.S. economy is in long-term trouble. In their view, the deficits mean that American companies and workers cannot compete against foreign ones, or that American products are being unfairly shut out of foreign markets. They also say that the country is going too deeply into debt and could get into trouble if foreigners stop lending it money to cover the deficits.

Other economists say that a deficit is not necessarily bad. In their view, it just means that the United States is more prosperous than the rest of the world and is buying more than it can make for itself efficiently, allowing Americans to get low-cost foreign products. The U.S. economy is very strong, they say, and foreigners will continue to lend it money for many years until the United States starts importing less and exporting more, which would cut the deficit.

Wine may be a small part of America's imports, but its export is important to wine-producing countries such as France, where vineyards can be seen in many parts of the country.

The Global Product

The more complicated a product is, the more likely it is to consist of a combination of parts and ideas from all over the globe, brought together by world trade.

Take a personal computer at your school, for example. The silicon chip that does the actual computing, the microprocessor, is probably made in the United States. But the computer's memory chips may come from Taiwan or Korea. The monitor may come from Mexico, the electric cables from China. The hard drive, the unit that stores information, probably comes from Singapore. Some of the software might have been created in India.

Airliners are also built with parts from all over the world. The Boeing 777 jumbo jet bears the name of the Boeing Company, whose headquarters are in Seattle, Washington. But companies in Canada, East Asia, and Europe help build the jet. About 20 percent of the parts in each plane, in fact, come from Japan.

The parts that make up cars come from all over as well: tires from one country, the engine from another, and the

Industrial Standards

Imagine if the world had 500 sizes of batteries. An American company that wanted to produce batteries would be confused—should we make size #426 or size #58? Which size do people in Europe want? Which size do people in Africa want? The company would end up making small quantities of many different types. That would be economically inefficient, raising costs of production. Batteries would be expensive.

To avoid this situation, companies agree on industrial standards. This means they build products that have standard sizes and designs. With a limited number of battery sizes sold in the world, companies can mass-produce them at low cost and be sure of finding customers. There is still room for competition: companies can try to make longer-life batteries, for instance.

Sometimes companies get together and agree on a standard. Other times, market competition determines the standard. A variety of products are offered and eventually people buy more and more of one and the others disappear. In the 1980s, two VCR standards—VHS and Beta—fought a battle like that in the United States. Eventually VHS won and Beta vanished from stores.

If you think about it, you can name quite a few products that are built to world standards: tires, floppy disks, electrical plugs, compact discs, photo film, and light bulbs are just a few.

body from yet another. Things have reached the point that you can't always say a product is "from" a particular country. Even products that have familiar American brand names may have been made entirely overseas.

Television sets are a good example. In the 1960s and 1970s, U.S. companies making TV sets at American factories faced intense competition from low-cost imports made in Asia. As a result, many U.S. companies stopped making TVs. Foreign companies such as Sony opened factories in the United States to build TV sets here. One of the last remaining American makers was the Zenith Electronics Corporation. But, to lower its costs of doing business, the company closed its U.S. factories in the early 1990s and moved production to Mexico. Mexicans built the sets, which were then shipped to the United States for sale.

So which sets were "American"? The Sonys, which were made in America by American workers but had a Japanese name? Or the Zeniths, which had an American name and design but were made by Mexicans? Nobody could really say.

Just as it's hard to say a product comes from a particular country, it can be hard to identify companies by nationality. Before the days of globalization, things were simpler. American companies were often 100 percent American. Their owners were Americans. They hired Americans to work in American factories to make products that were then shipped from American ports to reach foreign buyers. But today, that American company may open a factory in a foreign country and make products there, employing many foreigners. It might sell those products in that country or it might ship them back to the United States. The computer company IBM, for instance, has its headquarters in Armonk, New York. But it has factories, offices, and

Airplanes are a major American export. They also facilitate world trade. Today Boeing Aircraft like this 767 carry people, animals, and freight all around the world, including Pandas from China to the United States.

subsidiary companies (smaller companies that it owns) all over the world.

Changes in ownership are also eroding the national identity of companies. On stock markets in the United States, foreigners are free to buy shares of American-based companies, which make them part owners of the company. In the same way, Americans are free to buy shares of foreign-based ones. Sometimes an entire company is bought by a foreign company. The German car maker Daimler Benz now owns one of the largest car makers in the United States, the Chrysler Corporation. Chrysler has continued to make cars in the United States. But are they American cars if the company making them is owned by a German company and many of their components are coming from other countries? Again, no one can say.

This mix-up has occurred because companies are constantly on the lookout for the most economical places to build things. For products that require a lot of work by hand, such as shirts and dresses, that often means going to developing countries such as Guatemala and Vietnam, where wages are low. If the product requires a lot of advanced machinery and knowledge, such as a microprocessor, with millions of microscopic circuits in it, the United States is probably the low-cost location for the factory.

Companies don't just look at cost—they care about quality and reliability, too. For instance, even if wages are low in a particular country, companies do not want to put

New Currency: The Euro

In 1999 the European Union countries took a very dramatic step: each began to eliminate its own money. France began getting rid of the franc, Germany the deutschmark, Italy the lira. All would use a new kind of money, the **euro.**

They did it mainly to make trade simpler. Under the old system, when people in one of the 11 E.U. countries bought goods from one of the others, they had to change money. Now all 11 would use the euro and there would be no need to change. The 11 would be a single economic zone and become more efficient.

Imagine how complicated things would be if the 50 American states all used different money. If you lived in New Jersey and drove through Pennsylvania, you'd have to change money before you could stop for a hamburger. It's much simpler and more efficient that all 50 states use the dollar.

an important factory there if soldiers are fighting a civil war. The factory might be destroyed in an attack and the supply of the product cut off. Companies also do not want to locate in a country where workers are unskilled and turn out defective products. They will also stay away from countries where officials may ask for bribes, or where presidents don't last more than a few months in office. What if the current government is overthrown and the new government decides to confiscate all foreign factories?

To keep costs down and operations running smoothly, companies constantly shift their sources of products. A Korean company may come to an American computer maker and offer to make memory chips for less than the maker is currently paying to a company in Taiwan. So the computer company switches. A U.S. department store may stop buying shirts from a country because civil war has closed a shirt factory there. It is a constant battle of competition: which country can make a quality product at the cheapest price, and make it fastest? For workers in the companies, this constant change can be brutal. They may get good-paying jobs and raises if their country is on top in the competitive race, then lose their jobs if the country falls behind.

Over time, some countries are able to use this system to pull up their standard of living in dramatic ways. South Korea, for instance, went from being one of the world's poorest countries in the 1950s to one of its wealthier ones in the 1990s. South Korea and other countries in East Asia began their industrial climb by making low-skill products such as cheap toys and clothing for the world. As money came in from these sales and local workers became more skilled, the countries shifted to making more complicated and profitable things—cars and computer chips, for

It has become difficult to tell the difference between a foreign car and an American car. Foreign cars like this Honda may be made in the United States. American cars contain parts made in other countries.

instance. This was good news for the country's workers, because their wages rose. The manufacturing of toys and clothing shifted to other countries, such as Vietnam and Bangladesh, which were behind them in development.

Governments often compete for work. They try to attract international corporations to come to their countries to build factories and hire local people. Governments may offer special tax breaks or pay part of the cost of setting up a factory. Mexico, for instance, has been very successful in attracting U.S. companies to manufacture goods at special factories known as **maquiladoras,** which are allowed to send their products north across the border to American markets.

TRANSPACIFIC FLIGHT

IT'S A SMALL WORLD BY

PAN AMERICAN AIRWAYS

Travel posters lure travelers to foreign lands. Tourism has become the biggest form of trade for some countries. Tourists spending money contribute more to those economies than the exporting of goods.

Trade Isn't Just About Things

Until the 20th century, trade involved mostly physical products, things that you could touch, like cars, grain, and batteries. Today trade consists more and more of services. What this means is that people don't only *make* something for a foreign customer, they *do* something for that customer. In your own community, you can find many service jobs. People who fix your home's kitchen sink, install the cable TV hookup, or deliver your newspaper are all providing services, not making things. Service work becomes part of trade if the provider of a service is from one country and the customer is from another. It's a huge business: in 2000 the United States sold about $295 billion dollars worth of services to foreign countries, roughly one-third of its total exports.

One of the most important trade-related services is helping foreigners take vacations. The 50 million foreign visitors the United States hosted in 2000 spent about $85 billion while they were here. Now you might say, since all

Foreign Aid in the Global Economy

Loans are another important form of international commerce. Often countries that are short on money borrow from other countries.

But often countries borrow money and don't use it well. It might go to build a fancy palace for the president or to build an outmoded kind of factory. When this happens, the countries might have trouble paying back the loans. If many countries stop paying at the same time, this can mean serious problems for the world economy.

In 1997 Thailand, a country in Southeast Asia, began to have trouble repaying its many loans. An international panic resulted. Almost everyone to whom Thailand owed money suddenly wanted the money back, right away. Soon the same thing was happening to South Korea, Indonesia, Brazil, and Russia because of fears that those countries had problems like Thailand's. The more people wanted their money back, the more trouble the countries had, because they didn't have the money to pay everyone at once. An organization in Washington, D.C., called the **International Monetary Fund (IMF)** helped put together a rescue package of billions of dollars of new loans to keep those countries going until they could straighten out their economies and start generating money to repay their debts. Many people did lose their jobs in those countries, but a global meltdown that had been feared did not happen.

The Boeing Yankee Clipper opened the era of world travel by air when Pan American World Airways began flying between the United States, South America, and Asia in the 1930s. The "flying boat" carried 74 passengers and had a dining room and lounge.

this business takes place in the United States, how can it be trade? The answer is: because the customers are foreigners who come to the United States and pay for their vacations by changing foreign money into dollars. The effect on the U.S. economy is the same as any other kind of trade.

Another service that the United States sells is education. As a form of trade, it is a lot like tourism—foreigners come to the United States, not to take vacations but to learn. At university and college campuses all over the country, you can see foreign students in the classroom. They are in effect buying an American "product"—a good education.

Service trade also consists of selling brainpower. An architect in New York may get a request from a company in Singapore to design a glass office building. The architect provides the design and gets paid by the Singapore company. Or a banker in New York may carry out a financial

The United States also depends on visitors from other countries to help its balance of trade. Natural wonders such as the Grand Canyon draw tourists from overseas. New York City, Washington, and Florida are other popular tourist destinations.

transaction for a client in Turkey and collect a fee for this service.

Foreigners also provide services to Americans. The "MMX" technology that the Intel Corporation, a U.S. company, introduced in 1997 to speed up graphics and animation on personal computer screens was developed in Haifa, Israel. Teams of Israeli engineers at an Intel office in Haifa worked for many months to come up with the very complicated technology. They didn't make chips. Rather, they made a design that would allow factories elsewhere to make chips that would speed up the graphics.

Advances in telecommunications have helped move service jobs around the world, sometimes in surprising ways. These days when Americans dial toll-free customer-service telephone numbers, their calls are sometimes routed to a foreign country. An English-speaking employee answers the call, often sitting in a large call center with hundreds of people doing the same type of work. The employee deals with the problem and is paid with money from America.

Another huge kind of service trade involves granting of permission to do something. That may not sound like much, but the "something" may be the rights to use a famous brand name on a product or to put a particular type of production technology to work in a factory, or to reprint a best-selling novel. If you're traveling in a foreign country and you see familiar American brand names, it doesn't necessarily mean that the product was made in the United States. A local company may have made it and paid the American company for the right to put the well-known American name on it, so that it will sell well.

Yet another category of service trade is computer software. Countless CD-ROMs containing software for personal computers are shipped abroad from the United States each year. But the government officials who keep track of trade don't count them as physical products. This may sound strange, but as the officials see it, what's being paid for is permission to use the programs on those discs. That permission brings billions of dollars each year to American software companies.

A man burns a pair of GAP jeans while protesting the 1999 WTO conference in Seattle, Washington. The protestors claimed GAP exploits laborers in the third world.

Disagreement About Trade

Countries often get into arguments about trade. Country A might say that Country B is cheating on an agreement to open its market to foreign-made automobiles, causing Country A's auto makers to lose millions of dollars in sales. In the past, countries might have gone to war over disputes like these. Now, they would be more likely to send lawyers to the Geneva, Switzerland, headquarters of the **World Trade Organization (WTO)** to get a courtroom-style ruling on the dispute.

The WTO is an international organization with approximately 140 countries as members. Each country that joins the WTO promises to abide by the terms of tens of thousands of pages of trade agreements that the members have worked out together. These agreements are called the **General Agreement on Tariffs and Trade (GATT).** The basic principle of the GATT is that free trade is good and protectionism is bad. Governments should not impose high tariffs on foreign products, it says. They should not give money to their own industries to help them compete against foreign competitors that are more efficient. They should not have import rules that are so complicated that they tend to keep foreign products out.

But there are many exceptions to these rules. Poor developing countries are allowed to keep their markets more closed to foreign products than those of wealthy industrial countries. The rich countries often accept that when a poor country is trying to modernize its economy and raise its people's standard of living, it may want to protect local industries for a number of years. Often farm goods are protected from foreign competition, reflecting the fact that in many countries, the United States included, farmers enjoy great political influence with their governments.

Most disputes are worked out in negotiations between the two countries. Only if that doesn't work do they come to the WTO, where a three-member panel of trade experts listens to the specifics of the case, checks the pages of the GATT that apply, and makes a ruling on which side is right and which is wrong. In recent years, the United States has gone to the WTO to complain that the European Union unfairly favors bananas grown in former European colonies, hurting American companies' ability to sell bananas to Europe. The WTO ruled that Europe was at fault. Europe, meanwhile, complained that a special U.S. tax program amounts to unfair government help for U.S. companies selling abroad. Europe won that one.

When the WTO rules against a country, it issues a legal statement explaining its decision, similar to a U.S. Supreme Court decision. Usually the country that is found to be at fault changes the trade practice that got it into trouble. But it doesn't have to. Under WTO rules, a country can ignore a ruling against it. If it does that, it has to pay a price, sometimes in the form of sky-high tariffs imposed on its goods.

In the banana case, Europe wouldn't change its policies, so the United States put 100 percent tariffs on a range of European goods, including Italian cheese, British greeting cards, and French handbags. The idea was that the tariffs would make these goods so expensive that they'd be shut out of the U.S. market, causing the European companies making them to go to their governments and plead for a change to the banana policies.

As every country imposing tariffs soon learns, its own people suffer too. Keeping out those European products

Opening Japan to Baseball Bats

In the early 1980s, the United States spent three years negotiating with Japan about trade in aluminum baseball bats. The problem was that a big Japanese amateur league required that all bats sold to member teams have an official stamp of approval from the league. The league would not give American companies the stamp, so they could not sell their bats in Japan. The Japanese said the stamp's purpose was to make sure that all bats sold in Japan were safe and of high quality. American negotiators said that the stamp was a "non-tariff barrier" that was unfairly keeping American bats out of Japan. After long talks, Japan agreed to give the stamp to American companies and they were able to begin selling bats in Japan.

One of the causes of the worldwide economic slump in the 1930s was the trade barriers put up by the largest trading nations. High tariffs and tight restrictions put the brakes on business. Everything stopped like a huge traffic jam, throwing millions of people out of work and into bread lines for a handout of food.

means that Americans who like them can no longer buy them. Merchants in the United States whose business depends on selling these products to consumers may lose money or even go out of business. So sometimes the merchants go to the U.S. government to try to pressure it to call off the tariffs—or at least to put them on some other product.

Meanwhile, the other country may dig in its heels and decide that if its products are going to get hit this way, it's going to hit back. It retaliates by blocking imports from the first country and a **trade war** is underway. Usually trade wars end quickly. Neither side is happy because each is losing money, so they reach a deal.

There are other ways that countries make trade difficult. When the United States wants to put strong pressure on an unfriendly country, it may impose economic **sanctions** against it. This is an order that restricts American companies from trading with the country. An even stronger form of pressure is called an **embargo,** which stops trade with a particular country completely. Usually the target countries are ones that U.S. leaders feel pose a military threat to the United States or its allies. Over the years, the United States has placed sanctions on Cuba, North Korea, and Iraq.

The U.S. government says that sanctions will prevent the country from acquiring military technology. And because the sanctions will hurt the country's economy, they will cause the country's people to lobby their leaders to change the policies that the U.S. government does not like.

Sanctions are always controversial. Some people say they hurt only ordinary people in the target country, making them poorer, while the leaders remain in power and blame the outside country for the poverty. Others say that sanctions can serve a useful purpose. Many people believe, for instance, that sanctions applied against the old apartheid, or segregated, government of South Africa helped to bring white rule to an end and give full political rights to all people in that country.

World trade has been facilitated by the World Trade Organization, which has helped develop smoother trading relationships between countries of unequal stature. If a small country has a complaint against a big country, the WTO provides a neutral forum to hear the dispute. In former days, the small country would probably have just had to put up with the problem. The WTO sees itself as a

United Nations of trade where the countries of the world get together to solve their disputes peacefully and fairly.

But many people are unhappy with the WTO. They think that it considers only the interests of corporations and their profits and not ordinary people. In their view, the WTO doesn't care if trade means that workers get thrown out of their jobs or the environment is damaged. It only cares about whether trade can flow without restriction.

In the 1990s many environmentalists objected to a ruling that the WTO made against a U.S. environmental regulation that tried to protect sea turtles. The regulation said that any shrimp being brought into the United States had to be caught with a particular kind of net that is designed to make sure that turtles aren't swept up accidentally in the net and drowned. Several countries claimed it was too expensive for their fishing boats to buy the nets that the United States demanded, and that there were other effective ways of insuring that sea turtles weren't killed. The WTO decided that the U.S. rules were too restrictive and the United States should change them. In the critics' eyes, that showed that the WTO didn't care about the environment.

In the United States and other countries in the 1990s, a protest movement arose against the WTO. In 1999, when delegates from WTO countries met in Seattle, Washington, to discuss new ways to open markets, thousands of demonstrators paraded in the streets. Some of them tried to shut down the meeting by physically blocking the delegates from getting into the meeting halls. Police responded with tear gas. The protests were televised all over the country.

Those who oppose free trade have begun to have some effect in government. Many members of the Democratic Party began to support changing GATT rules so that trade policy would take into consideration worker rights and the

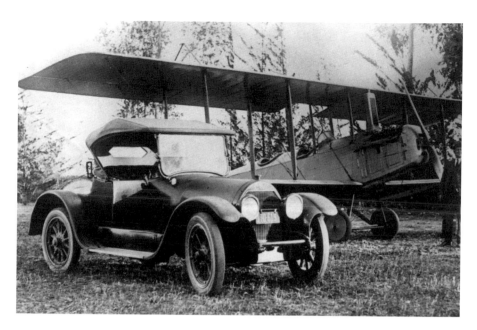

People who sneak something illegal into a country, or who do it to avoid taxes, are called smugglers. Smuggling is an ancient activity. In the 1920s smugglers used airplanes to carry illegal whiskey and alcohol into the United States.

environment. For example, if a country did not allow workers to form unions, or if it polluted the environment, it might be restricted in what it could sell to other countries.

Each day, everything you use, from your television set to the tangerines you ate for breakfast, may have come to you through a very complicated economic system that reaches into almost every corner of the globe. At the same time, products and services produced in your country went abroad to improve the lives of people in foreign countries. If current trends continue, trade will become an ever-bigger force in your life, helping determine what kind of job you get, how prosperous your family becomes, and where you live. Even if you never become an international traveler, you can be sure that each day the world will be coming to you.

Barter system—a means of trading without the use of money, in which goods or services are exchanged for other goods or services

Cold War—a conflict of ideological differences, especially between the United States and the Soviet Union

Communism—a philosophy advocating the elimination of private property so that all goods may be owned in common and available to all on an as-needed basis

Comparative Advantage—an economic theory that the world will produce the greatest amount of wealth if each country concentrates on making the products that it can make most efficiently

Embargo—a refusal by a country to sell goods to another country

Euro—the single currency that European countries began adopting in 1999 to make it easier to trade with each other

European Union—a group of European countries that have lowered barriers for trade with each other

Exports—goods that are sold outside of their country of manufacture

Foreign exchange—a type of money used in a foreign country; for example, Americans consider Japan's money, the yen, to be foreign exchange

Fair Trade—a philosophy that trade policies should take into consideration not just cost but such things as trade's impact on the environment and jobs that it may eliminate

Free Trade—a philosophy that products should be free to move from country to country without barriers

General Agreement on Tariffs and Trade (GATT)—the basic law of international trade; countries that are members of the World Trade Organization agree to obey its rules

Globalization—the interconnectedness of the world through communications technology and increased trade

Great Depression—A period during the 1930s when the U.S. economy was in severe decline, leading to widespread poverty and unemployment

Imports—foreign goods that are brought into another country for sale

International Monetary Fund (IMF)—a Washington-based bank owned by the governments of most of the world's countries; the IMF lends money to countries that are having trouble paying their debts

Internet—a network of computers that an individual with a personal computer can tap into to view information around the world

Labor unions—organizations that promote and protect the rights of workers

Maquiladoras—factories in Mexico that have special rights to ship their products to the United States and Canada

North American Free Trade Agreement (NAFTA)—An agreement between the United States, Mexico, and Canada to lower barriers to each other's products

Protectionism—a trade philosophy that says a country should prevent foreign products from coming in, to protect its own companies from foreign competition

Quota—a limit on the number of a particular type of foreign product that a country allows to come into its territory

Sanctions—coercive economic measures used to force a nation to do something

Standard of living—term used to describe how well individuals and families live in any given economy

Smoot Hawley Tariff Act—a U.S. law passed in 1930 to impose high tariffs on foreign products

Subsidy—financial aid that a government grants a business

Tariff—a tax that a government collects on foreign products that are brought into its territory; also known as a duty

Trade—the sale of goods and services made in one place to people in another place

Trader—one who makes a living by buying and selling goods

Trade barrier—a tariff, quota or any other law or practice that makes it hard for nations to sell their products abroad

Trade deficit—the financial gap that results if a country buys more from the outside world than it sells to it

Trade surplus—the financial gap that results if a country sells more to the outside world that it buys from it

Trade war—a conflict in which two countries that disagree about trade policies create trade barriers in an attempt to keep each other's products out

World Trade Organization (WTO)—a group that functions like a United Nations of trade; the WTO acts as a court to enforce trade rules that member countries have agreed to respect

Ballard, Robert D., with Rick Archbold. *The Lost Wreck of the Isis.* Charlestown, Massachusetts: The Horn Book, 1991.

Crane, Robert. *Understanding Today's Economics.* New York: Franklin Watts, 1979.

Jones, George. *My First Book of How Things Are Made.* New York: Cartwheel Books, 1995.

Langley, Andrew. *The Industrial Revolution.* New York: Viking, 1994.

Maestro, Betsy. *The Story of Money.* New York: Clarion Books/Houghton Mifflin Co., 1993.

O'Hara, Terence. *The Economy.* Philadelphia: Chelsea House Publishers, 2002.

Stimpson, Bea. *The World of Empire, Industry, and Trade.* United Kingdom: Stanley Thorne Publishers, 2000.

JOHN BURGESS is an editor at *The Washington Post.* From 1984 to 1987, he was *The Post's* correspondent in Japan and Korea, writing many articles about trade between the United States and Asia. In the 1990s, he lived in Washington, D.C., and covered trade. He is the great-great-grandson of an international trader, a Scottish chinaware merchant who moved to the United States in 1847.